Here's what people have to say about the Jannah Jewels Adventure Book Serie J

I can't continue without saying it one more time: ... g Muslim Girls! No damsels in dist... t, no cliché girly nonsense! ... This i... ow up reading.
–Emma Apple, Author of best... ns' Islamic Book Series

The Jannah Jewels books are awesome. They have made my daughters love to read with characters that dress like them and names they are familiar with. The stories keep their attention and make them curious about times past and present. We love Jannah Jewels at our house.
-Jessica Colon

The Jannah Jewels series are exactly what I would write if I had the gift of creative writing! As a mother, they are fun to read aloud as well as for the child to get immersed in! This series is the perfect blend of history, mystery, adventure and Islam! My daughter has even recommended these to her non-Muslim friends and was inspired to do a 'show and tell' on Mansa Musa thanks to these books! I'm thankful for these engaging stories and the strong female characters, thank you to the authors for a job well done, we can't wait for the rest of the series!
-Nazia Ullah

I like how you combine adventure and Islamic concepts to make us readers want to know more and more about the series. I am addicted to Jannah Jewels and I can't wait to find when and how they will get the artifact in America!
-Subhana Saad, Age 8

Fantastic book! My child was turning pages and couldn't wait to read the next chapter. So much so he's asking for the next book in the series.
-Mrs. S. A. Khanom, Book Reviewer

Our 8 year old had lost interest in reading and Jannah Jewels got her back to it. Not only that, this series has been our favourite gift to our children's friends and cousins and we hear children have a tendency to get hooked to these books!
-Umm Fatima

I have been reading Jannah Jewels for a long time and I love all the characters in this series. I can see myself in Hidayah and Iman, and I feel as if I'm in the actual story! I hope you love these books as much as I do!
-Fiza Ali, Age 10

I just wanted to thank you for these amazing books! I have 3 daughters, two of which are school age and they have recently been reading lots of Ninja Go books. We've been trying to find a better alternative for them to read and stumbled upon these, they are just wonderful! My girls are excited to read them, find them action filled and fun, while we don't need to worry about excessive violence or inappropriate language in the content. My life feels easier now thanks to these books, thank you SO much for your contribution to the Ummah, loving this series and we're looking forward to many books to come!
-Suzanne C.

My 8 year old has enjoyed these books immensely, she managed to finish each book in 2 days and has asked for more! We have made a small book club amongst our friends to swap and share the books, as mothers we love the strong role models the characters provide. We are looking forward to more books in the series!
-Falak Pasha

A captivating series with a rhythmic quest. Some of the books in the series also have surprises that made me jump into the next book right away. It's hard to put down, but at the same time I don't want to finish the book I'm reading unless there's another one waiting for me.
-Misbah Rabbani

We loved the Jannah Jewels books! There are very few Muslim books for kids that are entertaining. The Jannah Jewels books were very fun to read. They were so good that we read the entire series in two days!
-Zayd & Sofia Tayeb, age 10 & 7

I could really feel the love that went into this book – the characters, the places, the history, and the things that the author clearly strongly believes in and wants to share with our children and the wider world through her heroines…My daughter's verdict? "I would give the book a 10 out of 10 mum"
–Umm Salihah, HappyMuslimah.com Blog

I have a 9 year old boy and 5 year old girl. Both are very good readers now only because of Jannah Jewels. There are times when they were addicted to the screen. But Jannah Jewels changed everything upside down. The interesting characters, way of narration, adventure, artwork and messages make it more real in my kids' world and help them take the morals to heart. It changed their behavior a lot and made them good kids.
-Shaniya Arafath

My 8 year old loves this series - so much so that she has told all her friends about it, and one of them even gifted a couple more Jannah Jewels books for her birthday! In fact, I found myself reading her books much to the delight of my daughter - and then we both discussed our favorite parts. I love how the writers combine Islamic history with fun story lines and cute picture depictions. My daughter loves to sketch - and her books are filled with the Jannah Jewels character drawings. I would buy this series again and again. Thank you for all your wonderful work!
-Ruku Kazia

Learning about Islamic history and famous Muslims of the past makes these books a historical book lover's wish, and the Islamic twist is a plus for young Muslim readers. Jannah Jewels has been Muslimommy approved as kid-friendly!
-Zakiyya Osman, MusliMommy.com

I love all of the Jannah Jewels books, and the fact that you combine history and adventure in your stories. I also liked that you put the holy verses of Quran that remind us to stay close to Allah and I liked the fact that in one book you mentioned the verse from Quran which mentions the benefit of being kind to your enemy. I have read all of the Jannah Jewels books and even read two of these books in one day, that's how much I like these books!
–Fatima Bint Saifurrehman, Age 8

My kids liked the characters because they are modest in their mannerisms and dress, so that was something my daughter could relate to. Even though the characters are girls, it had enough excitement and the presence of supporting male characters to be read by both girls and boys. Throughout the book there was an essence of Islamic values and there was a lot of adventure to keep us guessing!
-HomeStudyMama, Book Reviewer

So inspirational... The young girls in these series are defined by the strength of their character. These non-stereotyped female role models are what our girls (& boys) need to read about. The storyline is engaging and subtly teaches moral lessons. Highly recommend these books.
-Amn, Book Reviewer

It's important for girls and boys, Muslim and not, to have strong, non-stereotyped female role models. Jannah jewels bring that in a unique way with a twist on time travel, fantasy, super heroes and factual Muslim history. It is beautifully written, engaging and an absolute must for any Muslim (and non-Muslim) kids library! My daughter LOVES The Jannah Jewels...
–Hani, Book Reviewer

We've reviewed 100s of Islamic non-fiction and fiction books from every single continent, except Antarctica, and none of the fiction books have made such an impression on our family as Jannah Jewels.
–Ponn M. Sabra, Best-selling author, AmericanMuslimMom.com

By Tayyaba Syed & Umm Nura

Vancouver

To Maariya, Amin and Hafsa: my very own God-given Jannah Jewels who brighten my days with their light and fill my heart with joy. Thank you for coming into my life. I love you. –T.S.

To Nura, Hanaan and Hakim: the coolness of my eyes, the light of my heart and the sparkle in my soul. Thank you for being you. 'I love you all the way up to the moon and back.' – U.N.

Published by Gentle Breeze Books, Vancouver, B.C., Canada

Copyright 2016 by Umm Nura
Illustrations by Clarice Menguito

Visit us on the Web! www.JannahJewels.com

ISBN:978-1-988337-01-2

August 2016

Contents

Sport:

Archery

Role:

Guides and leads the girls

Superpower:

Intense sight and spiritual insight

Fear:

Spiders

Special Gadget:

Ancient Compass

Carries:

Bow and Arrow, Ancient Map, Compass

HIDAYAH

Sport:

Skateboarding

Role:

Artist, Racer

Superpower:

Fast racer on foot or skateboard

Fear:

Hunger (She's always hungry!)

Special Gadget:

Time Travel Watch

Carries:

Skateboard, Sketchpad, Pencil, Watch

JAIDE

Sport:

Horseback Riding

Role:

Walking Encyclopedia,
Horseback Rider

Superpower:

Communicates with
animals

Fear:

Heights

Special Gadget:

Book of Knowledge

Carries:

Book of Knowledge, has
horse named "Spirit"

Sport:

Swimming

Role:

Environmentalist,
Swimmer

Superpower:

Breathes underwater for
a long time

Fear:

Drowning

Special Gadget:

Metal Ball

Carries:

Sunscreen, Water
canteen, Metal Ball

SUPPORTING CHARACTERS

JAFFAR

JASMIN

MASTER HORSERIDER

THE JANNAH JEWELS ADVENTURE 8

AMERICA

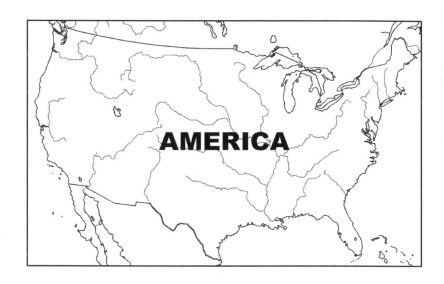

ARTIFACT 8: THE OPENING

"You must carry great humility and selflessness to lead others. Only then will you be followed."
~ The Old Master Archer

As salaamu alaikum Dear Readers,

Wow! The Jannah Jewels made it out of Turkey just in time!

Although they witnessed the victory in Constantinople, they had to return without an artifact. Now, in Book 8, they must figure out how to retrieve the 7th and 8th artifacts, as they embark on a brand new mission.

The Jewels arrive in America, learning what it means to always be of excellent character and never losing hope in Allah.

They meet Prince Ibrahima Abdur Rahman, who was captured and enslaved in West Africa and brought to America. Through his remarkable story of faith, humility and sacrifice, we see Islam as an important part of American history for centuries now.

Find out how the Jannah Jewels face an Adventure in America!

With warmest salaams,
Tayyaba Syed & Umm Nura

Prologue

Long ago, in the ancient Moroccan walled city of Fes, a decision was made. The great and peaceful Master Archer had reached old age and had to choose an apprentice to take his place and be trusted with the enormous task of protecting the world from the forces of evil. As Master Archer, he carried a deep Secret — one that no one else knew. To keep it hidden, the Secret was written upon a scroll, placed into a box and locked away in a giant Golden Clock. Who would keep this Golden Clock safe from the hands of evil after him? This decision would affect the future and balance of the world and had to be made with care and clarity.

He watched his students of archery very carefully, many of whom wanted to be chosen by their Master. Two of his students stood out to him like no other: Layla and Khan. Layla was flawless in her aim and light on her feet, who knew how to focus hard with her vision and her heart. She wanted nothing more than to bring peace into the world and use her skills in that way. Khan, on the other hand, was a fierce-fighter with strong hands and swift strategies and worked extra hard to gain his Master's attention. He had been practicing archery since he was old enough to hold a bow and learned the art from his older brother Idrees—a highly-trained senior student of the Master's.

The day finally came for the Master Archer to choose his successor and become the next Guardian of the Golden Clock and its Secret. Who would take on this great responsibility?

To everyone's surprise, he chose a woman to be the next Master Archer, the first time in history. Layla humbly accepted and continued to train relentlessly to prepare for this new role.

"Only those who are peaceful and know how to control their anger may possess the secrets of the Bow and Arrow," the Master Archer told all his students. "You must carry great humility and selflessness to lead others. Only then will you be followed."

Many of the Master's students respected and honored his decision, including Khan. He admired

Layla for her nobility and knew she must deserve this honor if the Master had chosen her over him and all the other students. Soon thereafter, he sent for her hand in marriage, and her family accepted.

The majority of the village rejoiced at their blessed union except for a few of the original Master's students. After the Master Archer announced his decision, this group of angry and disappointed students banded together and decided to leave the institution. Over time their anger turned into greed and jealousy. They spread rumors about Khan saying that he only married Layla to gain power and get his hands on the Golden Clock. They devised plans to separate the two great archers and steal the Clock along with its great Secret.

Layla and Khan were unaware of these terrible schemes. Khan went on to become a successful businessman and a leader of his community. The couple lived happily practicing the ways of the Bow and Arrow together whenever time permitted. They were blessed with two children: a boy named Jaffar and a girl named Jasmin. Jaffar was a gentle and curious spirit who loved to practice calligraphy and read as many books as he could. Jasmin was quite the opposite as she loved to play all kinds of sports, tumble and practice archery like her mother.

Khan had great expectations of his son and would push him to practice archery more. Jaffar was not a natural at it like Jasmin, nor had as much interest in it as her. To please his father, he would practice every day with Jasmin, although he just wanted to read and write. Jasmin enjoyed teaching her brother and loved being praised by her father. The family lived peacefully in their villa for some time until the day came that everything changed...

1

The Day Everything Changed

Idrees sat on the vinyl chair in the dark room staring at his little brother. It was hard for him to see Khan like this: so helpless and weak. Khan's helplessness reminded Idrees of how much he had to take care of Khan when they were younger. After their parents had suddenly died in a fatal car accident, Idrees had stepped up and taken care of his little brother like he was his own son. His teenage years turned into fatherhood as Khan was only a baby when the two brothers became orphans. He made sure to keep his baby brother happy no matter what.

He thought back to how happy Khan was with his wife Layla, how everything was perfect for them. He wanted more than anything for things to go back to the way they were again. Idrees' guilt ate him up every day. This is not how things were supposed to be.

After being hospitalized for weeks with a grade three concussion, Khan had finally arisen from his unconsciousness state after the bad fall. One of the Jannah Jewels had knocked Khan off his feet with a moving skateboard. Idrees knew it must have been a means of defense for the young girl, for Khan had entrapped the foreign kids wrongfully. Khan had become a different person ever since Idrees had solely made a harsh, life-changing decision for them all.

Once Khan had awoken from his concussion, he suffered from an extreme case of amnesia and kept having attacks of confusion and fear, not knowing who he was or where he was. The doctors decided to keep him sedated as much as possible for the stressful outbursts were affecting the condition of his heart. He needs more time to heal and rest, they had told a saddened Idrees. They hoped the amnesia was only a temporary side effect of the concussion.

But, there was no way Idrees could have predicted things would have spiraled into such a mess. If only he had not sent *her* away. If only he had not separated them. Had he been too rash in his decision? What else could he have done? There was no other choice that dreadful day. That was the day that everything changed…

Idrees and Khan had just returned from a business trip. It was Khan's habit to see his family first as soon as he came back to Fes. The two brothers arrived and found Khan's children practicing archery together in the field behind their house. The sky was clear with a bright sun shining over the tall brick walls surrounding the grounds. They watched as Jaffar had an arrow locked in his bow aiming at a target some feet away. Khan was adamant to oversee Jaffar's progress, but Idrees knew his nephew would get nervous around his father.

And just as Jaffar realized his father was watching, he missed his target and sent his arrow flying into a tree behind it. He squinted his eyes and braced himself as he must have known what was coming.

"Jaffar!" Khan said unhappily. His tall, lean body towered over his little son. "You must learn to focus, boy! Were you even looking at the target?"

Jaffar squeezed the grip of the large bow hard with his hand, flared his nostrils, and bunched his lips together. Idrees saw Jaffar keep his gaze down and not answer his father.

"Father, he was doing fine before you came," Jasmin tried to speak up, but Khan ignored her.

"When are you going to learn to aim right?" Khan kept his dark eyes looking down on Jaffar angrily. Idrees listened as Khan raised his voice in frustration.

"Greetings of Peace, Khan, and Brother Idrees," Khan's wife Layla had just joined them in the back field. "Khan, please go easy on Jaffar," she advised him. "He's only seven years old." She carried a tray of drinks and set them onto the patio table and hugged Jaffar.

Idrees noticed Khan suddenly soften up.

"He's been practicing for years now, Layla," Khan said with a deep sigh. "I know he can do better."

"He will with time, not with haste," she replied in a gentle way. She bent down and grabbed Jaffar's face. "Come. Have a drink. You and your sister have been practicing all afternoon. I made your favorite lemonade with a touch of fresh apple mint leaves," said Layla with a warm smile.

Jaffar then turned and noticed his Uncle Idrees. Instantly, Jaffar ran over to him.

"Uncle!" Jaffar exclaimed as he hugged him tight. Idrees loved to see Jaffar happy.

"Jaffar! My boy! You're getting taller by the minute. Soon you'll be as tall as me," he said laughingly. Idrees grabbed Jaffar's hand and walked over to the others. "Peace be upon you, Sister Layla," Idrees greeted.

Jasmin then got up to hug her uncle shyly.

"And who is this beautiful young lady?" Idrees asked as he lifted her chin up to look at him. Both his niece and nephew had a special place in his heart.

"It's me, Jasmin," she answered flashing her smile with missing teeth.

"Oh! I didn't recognize you, my dear. I see you lost another tooth!"

"Yes, just yesterday! You see that tree over there?" Jasmin said as she pointed towards the tree with Jaffar's arrow stuck in its trunk. "I climbed it all the way to the top, found the reddest apple I could find and bit into it and then my tooth got stuck in it and then there was blood everywhere!"

Uncle Idrees bellowed a deep laugh.

"That's enough now, Jasmin," Layla said. "Drink your juice quickly and then run along inside and grab a snack. Make sure to wash your hands first."

"Yes, Mother," Jaffar and Jasmin mumbled. They sat and drank up, then headed into the house disheartened to leave their beloved uncle.

"Any news, Brother Idrees?" Layla asked as soon as the kids were out of sight.

Idrees took a seat, and Layla and Khan followed. "It's not good," he said with seriousness and concern, taking a few sips of the lemonade. "I have been telling Khan that there are rumors going around about you two. I'm worried that some people might want to come after you both and try to steal the 'you-know-what'," he spoke as softly as he could.

"Let them say what they want about us," Khan said passively. "We know the truth. That's all that matters. And as far as the 'you-know-what,' Layla has hidden it away. There's no way they can get to it."

Layla was quiet for a few moments.

"Something doesn't feel right," she said with worry. "People can do anything for power—even if it means harming..." but before she could finish her sentence a sharp *'whoosh'* sound sliced through the air right past her. An arrow had landed in the center of the patio table. She suddenly stood up and looked around. "There must be intruders here! Get inside!"

"Brother, get the bows!" shouted Khan as he pulled him and Layla under the patio table. Idrees yanked the metal tray off the table sending empty lemonade glasses flying. He shielded himself with it and bolted towards the house. Arrows flew at him from the surrounding trees like buzzing bees. He rushed in and grabbed three bows and a case of arrows from Khan's equipment room.

"Uncle Idrees, what's wrong? What's happening?" Jasmin ran down from upstairs in a panic.

Idrees grabbed her by the shoulders. "Listen to me very carefully. Go back upstairs, grab your brother, and play hide-and-seek in the crawl space in your father's closet. Do not make a sound. I will come and find you very soon like I always do. Do you hear me?" His eyes were wide and red.

"But…," Jasmin stalled trying to get a glimpse of the backyard.

"Go, child! NOW!"

Jasmin shook from the sound of Idrees' command and ran back up without anymore questioning. He had never yelled at her before.

He ran to the back door and saw Layla and Khan shielding themselves with the patio table which was flipped over on its side. They were out of breath with their backs leaned against it.

"Khan, here!" Idrees said as he was about to

toss a bow to him.

"No, don't!" Khan stopped him. "We will get hit before we even release the arrow. Just stand guard! We need to get inside."

Idrees rapidly fired arrows from behind the patio door. It was like shooting into thin air with no aim in sight as the intruders were camouflaged deep within the high, thick-leaved trees that hovered over the grounds' tall brick walls.

Khan tried to shield Layla from getting hit as he rolled the round table along with her. Idrees watched as Khan suddenly buckled to the ground. "Aaahhh!" Khan yelled in pain. An arrow had pierced through his calf.

"Khan!" Layla shouted as she looked back at her wounded husband.

"Little brother!" screamed Idrees. His heart sank as he watched his brother squirm miserably behind the table.

"Go! Go! Go!" Khan ordered Layla. "Get inside!"

Layla's face was wet with tears.

"No! I'm not leaving you!"

"Brother, pull her inside with the bow!" Khan was on his knees holding up the table with both arms.

Idrees squatted and held one end of the long bow stretching it towards Layla. "Grab hold!"

"Khan, no!" Layla protested.

"There's no time to waste! Go now!" he yelled with whatever might he had left.

Layla reached for the other end of the bow and let Idrees pull her in as she army-crawled towards him. She cried as she reluctantly inched her way into the house. "Brother Idrees! Khan's been hit! We need to save him! Please!" she pleaded as she slowly stood up.

"I will save my brother, but after I have fully saved you. *You* must escape at once!" Idrees spoke assertively as he panted.

"What? No! Never!" Layla's face was stern with shock. "How can I leave my husband, my children, my home? Give me that bow! I'll save Khan myself!"

Idrees held the bow tight as Layla tried to yank

it out of his hand. "Dear Sister, listen to me! You are the Master Archer! If these intruders don't get you today, they surely will another day. You're the only one who can access the Secret in the Golden Clock! The world is depending on you. We can't risk anything happening to you. You must leave right now. Take the secret passage and get as far away from here as you can!"

"Help me!" Khan's voice echoed in from outside.

Idrees looked out the door. Khan was only a few feet away from the house crawling slowly towards them as he dodged showering arrows from the sky. Idrees noticed a trail of red etched onto the concrete patio floor behind Khan.

"He's bleeding!" Layla screamed with terror.

"GO!" Idrees demanded.

Layla's cry was piercing. She shook with sadness. He watched as Layla ran down the long corridor towards the basement door. She turned and looked at Idrees with one last silent plea of desperation.

Idrees gestured her to keep going. He will never

16

forget the broken-hearted stare Layla gave him as she escaped with swollen, water-filled eyes.

"Brother!"

Idrees quickly turned back towards Khan and bent forward reaching his hand out to pull his brother into the house. Khan moaned in pain as his body dragged over the threshold of the back door frame. Idrees slammed the door shut as fast as he could and then checked Khan's leg.

"Where's the arrow?" he asked in astonishment.

"I—pulled—it—out." Khan could barely speak.

Tears ran down Idrees' cheeks. He tore off a piece of fabric from the bottom of his long robe. He quickly wrapped the wound putting immediate pressure on it. "Don't worry, Brother. You are going to be okay." Idrees withdrew his cell phone from his pocket and dialed the emergency number for help.

Khan's eyes were closed as he lay in his brother's arms listening.

As soon as Idrees hung up, Khan asked, "Where is my Layla? Is she okay?" His voice was but a whisper.

Idrees remained silent.

"Brother, answer me."

"She's…gone…I…I told her to leave," Idrees' spoke faintly, his voice shaking.

Khan opened his eyes big. "Leave? Why?!"

"She needs to get to safety. We can't risk something happening to her. This was too close."

"No! Stop her!" Khan begged. "She can't leave. I'll continue protecting her! How could you make her do this? How could you just let her leave us? How could you just let her leave *me*?!" Khan's voice pierced Idrees' ears as he cried uncontrollably.

"I'm sorry, Little Brother. It was the only choice."

Khan's face suddenly stiffened with anger. With wet, blood-shot eyes and flushed skin, he stared hard at Idrees. His body shook from the trauma of his injury. "I will never forgive you for this, Brother. Never." The words spit out of Khan's mouth.

Idrees' heart immediately ached. Before he could protest, Khan passed out.

2

Time Crunch

Sensei Elle bunched her eyebrows together. Her gray eyes were wide with shock. "Stolen?!"

Hidayah, Iman, Jaide and Sara immediately lowered their gazes as no one knew how to answer her.

"What do you mean the seventh artifact was stolen?" she uttered her words slowly and firmly as if the concept was unfeasible.

The Jannah Jewels looked up at Hidayah fretfully. Iman gave her a quick nod to speak up on behalf of all of them.

"Umm...Sensei, Jasmin showed up at the end of our mission. She tried capturing Sara, but her attempt failed. However, she did manage to steal the 7th artifact from her," Hidayah spoke with hesitation.

The color left from Sensei's face. It suddenly became stiff and grim. "Jasmin?" she whispered. Hidayah sensed sadness in Sensei's voice, whose eyes seemed lost and distant in that moment.

"Yes, Sensei, it was Jasmin," Sara spoke up softly. "She snatched it right out of my hand. I couldn't stop her."

Sensei leaned against the inside wall of the tree with disbelief. She lowered her head and closed her eyes for a few moments. The Jewels could see her lips moving as she uttered a quiet prayer. None of them could make out her words.

She slowly opened her eyes that glistened with wetness inside the tree's dim candlelight.

I wonder why she is so taken aback, Hidayah thought to herself.

"You must retrieve the 7th artifact immediately," Sensei told the Jewels. "The Golden Clock will malfunction if the artifact is not found soon."

"Sensei, our two helpers Jaffar and Mus'ab from Fes met us in Turkey and said they would get it back for us from Jasmin," Jaide decided to speak up now.

Sensei Elle's disposition quickly changed. She nodded a few times in deep thought. "And how will they get it to you in time?"

Hidayah hesitated a bit before answering. "We figured we could all meet on the next mission." She paused to check Sensei's reaction, but her expression was neutral. Hidayah then continued, "Is that possible? Can we go on the next mission even though we haven't gotten the 7th artifact?"

Sensei looked at each of the Jewels' faces. They all stood taut anticipating her response. "This has never happened before," she told them. "We will have to make do despite our current circumstances. Jaide, may I see your time-travel watch? It can help us see how much time we have to complete the next mission."

Jaide gulped as she looked at the other Jewels. She quickly swung and hid her wrist behind her back. "I'm sorry, Sensei. I can't give it to you."

"What? Why not?"

Jaide avoided making eye contact. "Please don't be upset. I don't know how it happened, but—it—stopped—working back in Constantinople," Jaide's words dragged out of her mouth. "We are just grateful we still made it back in time—thanks to God."

"Yes, Allah was surely protecting you through all these challenges on your last mission," Sensei responded. She then put her empty palm out towards Jaide. "Please hand it to me, Jaide. We must fix it right away."

Jaide slowly brought her wrist back forward. She unfastened the watch and handed it to Sensei Elle.

The girls all watched as Sensei quickly examined it, flicking it lightly with the nail of her index finger. She then brought it close to her ear and shook it. "It looks as if the battery may need to be changed," she speculated. "I hope it's just that, God-willing. I will quickly head up to the dojo and try to fix it. In the meantime, go gather up some energy then meet me back at the dojo soon."

"Yes, Sensei," the Jannah Jewels all responded simultaneously. They headed out to each of their homes agreeing to reconvene shortly.

*   *   *   *

As the sun shined behind her, Hidayah sluggishly rode her bike back home. So many thoughts rushed through her mind. *How did all this even happen?* she wondered. After everything they went through on their last mission, Hidayah could not fathom how they returned empty-handed without the artifact. She gravely worried how Jaffar and Mus'ab would get it from Jasmin. She never wanted to put them in such a predicament.

What if they can't find Jasmin? What if she destroys the artifact before they do find her? What if they get hurt in the process? What if they can't make it to the next mission? Hidayah grew more and more anxious as she neared her house. Her bike's handlebars became slippery from her sweaty hands. She carefully dried each palm against her dress.

Oh Most Merciful God, please forgive us for our shortcomings and do not be displeased with us.

Accept us and direct us only towards good, Hidayah prayed in her heart.

A sense of relief came over her as she pulled up to her driveway. She was happy to finally be home. She stepped off her bike and punched in her garage code, then walked her bike into an empty corner.

The house was fully lit from all the natural light that poured in through the many windows. It was nice-sized and roomy for Hidayah and her aunt and uncle. She walked into the warm kitchen and saw her Aunt Khadija cooking. She greeted her from behind.

"Peace be upon you too," her aunt turned and replied. She froze at the sight of Hidayah. "That must have been some party. You look exhausted."

Hidayah quickly grabbed the toaster off the counter and caught a glimpse of her reflection. She could not believe her eyes which were red with dark circles underneath them. She realized her worries were written all over her face.

"Yes, it was," Hidayah did not know how else to answer her Aunt Khadija.

"Well, you are just in time to join me for some

tea. Come. Have a seat."

Hidayah met her aunt on the kitchen table. She poured two cups of steaming tea, serving one to her aunt on a silver tray just the way Sensei had taught her to treat her elders.

"So, tell me about the party," said Aunt Khadija. "Did Jaide like her gift?"

After dunking a biscuit gently into her tea cup, Hidayah answered, "She loved the new sketchpad." She then took a bite. "Her parents got her an electric skateboard, which we took for a spin," Hidayah said with a smile. *Spin is an understatement*, she thought back to how useful it was on their last mission during the Conquest of Constantinople.

"That sounds like fun," said her aunt. "You girls are so good for each other, plus Sensei Elle has been such a great mentor for you all. You must stick with her, okay? Good company is a blessing from above."

Hidayah absorbed her aunt's words as she took some slow sips of her tea. She stared out the window remembering how she was so drawn to

25

Sensei Elle when she first saw her and then recalled all the amazing people the Jewels had met on their missions thus far. Her heart was finally feeling somewhat at ease at this point.

The house phone rang just then. Aunt Khadija stood up to go answer. Hidayah took some final sips of her now-lukewarm tea. As she walked her empty cup and plate to the sink, her aunt brought the phone to her.

"It's Sensei," she informed Hidayah. "She wants to talk to you. Sounds urgent," her aunt said handing her the phone.

Hidayah took the phone and greeted Sensei.

"Hidayah, listen very carefully," Sensei sounded incredibly troubled. "You and the other Jewels need to come to the dojo at once. We don't have much time."

A sudden rush of worry came over Hidayah. "Yes, Sensei. Be right there." She hung up the phone and quickly dialed each of her friends telling them to get to the dojo right away.

"Everything okay?" asked her aunt.

"I think Sensei needs help with something at the dojo. I'll be back soon, God-willing," Hidayah quickly changed into her red sweatshirt and joggers. She kissed her aunt's cheek, slipped on her sneakers and ran out of the house with her bow and arrow in hand and the bamboo case with the ancient map over her shoulder.

"Be home before dark!" her aunt called out distantly behind her.

"Okay!" Hidayah shouted back. Her sneakers pounded against the pavement as she raced up the hill. She arrived at the dojo first, then Iman, Jaide and Sara arrived shortly thereafter.

They all stood in a huddle trying to catch their breaths.

"What's going on?" asked Iman as she slid her glasses back up her sweaty nose.

"I was in the middle of my egg noodle soup. This better be important," Jaide whined.

"You know Sensei would only call us if it's important," reminded Sara.

"Yes, thank you for coming so quickly." The Jewels spun around to look at Sensei, who met them on the front porch. "I'm sorry you were not able to rest for long. I fixed the watch and look at what it says," she lifted the time-traveling watch to show its face, which was pointing at the number 5.

"What does that mean?" asked Iman.

"It means you only have 5 hours to complete the next mission!" Sensei answered abruptly.

Sara gasped and covered her mouth with both her hands. The Jannah Jewels all stared wide-eyed at the watch in disbelief.

Hidayah knew what she had to do. She quickly made a silent prayer in her heart. *Oh Lord, You are the Creator of time. Please help us bring back both the seventh and eighth artifacts to the Golden Clock in enough time.*

3

Departure

"Is that enough time?" Jaide questioned. "Even if we somehow manage to find the 8th artifact, what if Jaffar and Mus'ab don't get the 7th one to us in time? And how do you even get in touch with them to let them know of the time crunch?"

"You must leave at once for your next mission," instructed Sensei. "There is no time to waste. Focus on getting the 8th artifact for now." She handed the watch to Jaide who quickly placed it back on her wrist.

"Can you tell us where we are headed and which artifact we need to retrieve, Sensei? That will cut down our time a lot," Iman insisted.

"Follow me," she said quickly heading towards the field behind the dojo.

As the girls trailed behind Sensei, Jaide leaned in forward to whisper into Sara's ear, "I didn't even get time to charge my skateboard. It's still dead. Nor did I get to separate Mus'ab's board from mine. I left both at home. How can we go on the next mission without the boards?"

Sara partially looked back over her right shoulder. "I don't know. Some things definitely seem off about this mission, but I trust Sensei. She wouldn't send us if she didn't think we were ready," she reassured Jaide.

They entered a fenced grassy area and found Shams, the goat that had followed the Jewels from Morocco, sitting by herself.

"Why does she look so down?" asked Hidayah.

Iman walked up to Shams and squatted down to stroke her orange coat. "What's wrong, sweetie?" but Shams sat quietly without much motion.

"She has not been eating or drinking much," Sensei informed them as she approached the sad-looking goat. "You will be meeting a famous Prince on this mission. You must take Shams with you, so he can bring her back to good health," she told them.

The Jannah Jewels had met a few members of royal families on previous missions. They were aware of the proper manners required of them when around royalty.

"And where will we find him?" asked Jaide, expecting to go to another far away land.

Sensei stood with her hands tied in front of her. "In America," she answered calmly.

"America?!" Jaide was stunned. "There's royalty in America?" she questioned.

"Yes. Don't forget you are going back in time. You will find the ancient artifact at the hands of the Prince. It is very soft and white, but be careful as it is very fragile. In order to retrieve it, you must give him a gift first," said Sensei.

"Wait. What's the artifact, and what do we have to gift him?" Iman questioned. "We don't have anything to give him," she stated.

"The eighth artifact is the Opening," answered Sensei Elle.

"Uhh, the opening to what?" Jaide questioned. "I'm so confused. A Prince? America? The Opening? Can't you just tell us, Sensei?" she insisted.

"There is no time to explain. Hidayah, use your ancient map to guide you, and Iman, use your *Book of Knowledge* to find your answers," Sensei hastened them as she lifted Shams into her arms. She hurried down the hill, her long red robe picking up the wind and swaying behind her. The Jannah Jewels gathered their belongings and followed right after her.

None of the Jewels expected to arrive back at their favorite maple tree so soon. They never had such a short gap between missions before. Despite this, they overcame their weariness and were ready to take on the next big task for they knew it was all for the greater good.

Sensei Elle handed Shams to Iman. "Take good care of her and stick together," she told the Jewels. "Allah places you where He sees fit as He is the Best of Planners. May He guide your every step towards Him."

The Jannah Jewels pushed the tree trunk and slid down, down, down. They formed a circle holding each other's hands. Iman hugged Shams in one arm and held Hidayah's hand with the other. They closed their eyes and recited together in unison, *"Bismillah hir Rahman nir Raheem."*

4

Frenemies

Mus'ab sat under his argan tree and stared up at Jaffar. They both were winded and exhausted. "Where are we going to find your sister?" Mus'ab asked.

Jaffar stood atop the hill and looked down to the great walled city of Fes. "She could be anywhere," he replied. His eyes scanned the many streets and rooftops below.

"Don't forget the hawk knocked her off her horse. She couldn't have gone too far if she's injured," Mus'ab pointed out.

Suddenly, it dawned on Jaffar where Jasmin could be. "The hospital!" He pulled Mus'ab up by the hand, and the two ran down the hill to Mus'ab's house. They grabbed Mus'ab's brothers' bikes and rode through the busy narrow streets heading slightly outside Fes el Bali to Omar Drissi Hospital.

Their pedals spun rapidly as they weaved through the crowd making sure to not run into any pedestrians or cars. Mus'ab's legs began to ache which were still sore from the last mission, especially his limped leg. It was quite a distance via bicycle to get to the hospital. He did his best not to lose sight of Jaffar, but he quickly grew tired. He pulled over to the side of the road under a tree to catch his breath. He wished they had brought some water with them.

Jaffar soon gained a big lead. He turned back and saw Mus'ab a good distance behind him. As Mus'ab panted with fatigue, he waved to Jaffar to keep going.

"I'll meet you there!" he cupped his hands around his mouth and yelled as loud as he could to Jaffar. Jaffar gave him thumbs up and continued riding.

As he approached the hospital, he slowed down and carefully steered the bike underneath the portico entrance of the hospital. He quickly tied it against a bike rack a few meters away and then ran towards the revolving doors.

Suddenly, he heard footsteps charging after him, and then he was floating off the ground. He was lifted off his feet and pulled up by his arms. Jaffar looked to his immediate right then left and to his surprise, found that Moe and Slim were yanking him by each arm and dragging him away to a side alley near the hospital.

"Moe! Slim! What are you doing? Where are we going?" Jaffar was completely baffled at their behavior. They released him pushing him hard against the brick wall of the alley. Jaffar's back pounded against the wall knocking the wind out of him. He took a minute to collect himself as his pain subsided. He looked up at Moe and Slim with disbelief. "What's wrong with you two?!"

Moe and Slim stared hard at their old friend as they took heavy breaths. Their eyebrows were bunched together, and their eyes bulged with anger.

"How dare you show your face here?" Moe

shouted, his nostrils flaring back and forth.

"I need to find Jasmin! She stole the seventh artifact, and I need to get it back to the Jannah Jewels right away!" Jaffar told them hastily.

"So you *are* working for the Jannah Jewels now, aren't you?" the words spit out of Slim's mouth as he towered over Jaffar. "*You* are the reason Jasmin broke her arm so badly and is in this hospital in the first place. She told us how you've joined the Jewels and turned against your own sister! What kind of brother are you?"

Jaffar could not believe what he was hearing. "I would never deliberately cause harm to my own sister! I haven't even seen her in over a month!"

Moe leaned in real close to Jaffar. "Save it!" he yelled as he stabbed his pudgy finger into Jaffar's chest. "You are not to go anywhere near Jasmin, and we are going to make sure of that."

Jaffar felt like he was in a bad dream. How could his friends turn on him like this? "You guys need to listen to me," he pleaded trying to sound as sensible as possible. "There is no time to waste. I have to see her right now. If you don't trust me, then take me to her."

Slim arched his lanky body. "You need to get as far away from this hospital as possible—now!"

So many questions raced through Jaffar's mind. He could not understand why Jasmin would turn his closest friends into his enemies or how he could get through to them at this point. But this was not the time to figure all this out. He knew he had to get out of this mess right now but how? He wished Mus'ab was with him. Then, it suddenly dawned on him.

Mus'ab must be nearby by now, he thought to himself.

"Mus'ab! Help!" Jaffar screamed as he tried to push through Moe and Slim with all his might.

Within a few moments, they heard a loud whistle from the opposite end of the wet alley. Moe and Slim quickly turned back startled by the noise. Mus'ab was charging at them on his bike. Jaffar saw his moment out and squirmed through them. He escaped their huddle and ran as fast as he could away from them.

"Hey! Get back here!" Slim shouted as him and

5

Broken

Jaffar felt utterly hurt and confused. "I don't know why Jasmin turned them against me," he said sadly.

"Is she in this hospital?" asked Mus'ab.

Jaffar nodded.

"Let's go and find her then. We need to get the seventh artifact back to the Jewels before it's too late. Forget those guys for now. I soaked them good with muddy water," said Mus'ab.

Jaffar's gray eyes absorbed Mus'ab's words carefully. "Okay, let's hurry." He realized there was no time to waste. The boys ran into the hospital and went straight to the front-desk. They asked for Jasmin Khan's room number and were directed to the fifth floor pediatrics unit. They took the nearest elevator up.

As the elevator doors slid open, the boys busted through almost knocking over a heavy-set man.

"Whoa! Slow down there!" the old man yelled almost falling over.

"Uncle Idrees?" Jaffar stared at his uncle in disbelief.

"Jaffar! My boy!" his uncle suddenly smiled as he grabbed Jaffar and squeezed him hard.

Mus'ab stood and watched the two embrace for a long time.

Finally Uncle Idrees released Jaffar out of the hug and looked at him with relief and contentment. "I'm so glad you're okay. You had us worried sick for the last few weeks," he told Jaffar. "Where have you been?"

Jaffar turned and looked at Mus'ab then back at his uncle. "Uncle Idrees, this is my good friend Mus'ab. I've been staying with him and his family. He and I have been working together to help the

Jannah Jewels. We're here to find Jasmin, who stole the seventh artifact from them."

"Yes, I recently came to know of this," said Uncle Idrees. "I just came from her room. After much questioning, she finally told me that she did have it but then got rid of it."

Both Jaffar and Mus'ab stared in shock.

"No!" Jaffar exclaimed. "Where is she? I'm sure she still has it! I'll get it out of her."

"Jasmin is not well, Jaffar." Uncle Idrees told him. "She reinjured her arm very badly, and this time has fractured both bones in her forearm. They will be taking her in for surgery very soon."

"Uncle, please. We have to get that artifact back to the Jewels immediately. I just need to talk to her for a few minutes. She will listen to me. I'm sure of it." Jaffar's eyes searched his uncle's for agreement.

Uncle Idrees let out a deep sigh. "Come with me," he told the boys.

The three of them walked through the pediatric unit which was full of colorful and playful murals on its walls and decorative figures hanging from the ceiling. The hospital staff smiled and greeted Uncle Idrees as if he was a usual on the floor. He led them to a corner room with a glass door shielded by a white curtain. Uncle Idrees knocked on the door and slid it open.

"May I come back in, Jasmin?"

"Yes," a soft voice spoke out from behind the curtain.

Uncle Idrees signaled Jaffar to follow him in.

"Wait here," Jaffar whispered to Mus'ab. As he walked around the curtain, Jaffar's heart grew heavy with worry at the sight of his sister. She was lying on her bed, tired and swollen. She wore a hospital gown which exposed her broken arm. It was black and blue and looked completely displaced. She looked like she was in pain and very uncomfortable. In that moment, Jaffar felt sorry for his little sister.

As soon as Jasmin saw her brother, she raised her head and neck and glared at him with piercing eyes.

"How did *you* get in here?" she questioned him

angrily.

Jaffar took a second to speak. "How are you feeling?"

Jasmin looked up at her uncle. "Please tell him to leave. I don't want him near me."

Uncle Idrees placed his large hand on her shoulder. "Jasmin, my dear. We can't disregard family like this. He is your older brother. Be respectful."

"Ha! Family? Brother?" Jasmin mocked his words. "I know why he is here. He could care less about me. He is more worried about helping those awful Jewels and retrieving the artifact for them. Don't tell me the importance of family! He's the one that betrayed Father and me!"

"Father kidnapped those poor kids, Jazz! That was wrong of him and wrong of you not to object to his actions!" Jaffar could feel himself getting hot.

Suddenly, Uncle Idrees' cell phone began to vibrate in his pant pocket. He pulled it out and looked at its screen worriedly. "I must take this call. I'll be right back," he said as he quickly stepped out of the room.

"Wait! Take Jaffar out of here!" Jasmin pleaded, but Uncle Idrees had already exited. She dropped her head back onto the bed grunting hard. "You better leave now, Jaffar, or else!" she warned him.

"Or else what? You going to turn Uncle Idrees against me too just like you did with Moe and Slim?" Jaffar's face was tight with anger. "Haven't you suffered enough for your wrong actions? Now tell me where the artifact is!" He leaned in close to her bedside.

Jasmin shoved him away with her good arm. "I don't have it! Now leave me alone."

"Liar!" Jaffar shouted. "I know you came straight to the hospital after you returned from Turkey. What did you do with it?"

"If you don't leave, I am going to scream," Jasmin threatened.

"You wouldn't."

She gave him a look of defiance. "Wait until Father is better. Then you will truly be sorry. Now, get—OUT!" Jasmin squealed at the top of her lungs.

Within moments, nurses and hospital staff came

running into Jasmin's room.

"What's going on in here?" questioned a head nurse wearing a white headscarf. "Jasmin, are you okay? Who is this boy?" The nurse glared at Jaffar disapprovingly.

"I am her brother," he answered softly.

"No, he is not," Jasmin replied abruptly. "Please get him out of here." She turned her face away from him.

To hear those words from his own sister felt sharper than a knife piercing through his skin. He looked at her in disbelief—hurt—stunned.

She refused to look back at him.

"I'm afraid you can't be in here, young man," said the head nurse. "Do I need to call security?"

"There is no need. I'll let myself out," Jaffar dragged his feet as he disappointedly walked out of the room. He sluggishly walked over to Mus'ab who was sitting by a set of water fountains. He immediately stood up as Jaffar approached him.

"What happened?"

"Let's go," Jaffar told him avoiding eye contact. "I don't want to be here any longer."

"What about the artifact?" Mus'ab questioned with worry.

"She doesn't have it," answered Jaffar feebly.

"And you believe her?"

Jaffar shrugged his shoulders. "I don't know what to believe. She also said I wasn't her brother." The words still stung.

"Dude, get it together!" Mus'ab shook Jaffar's shoulders. "If we don't find this artifact and get it back to the Jewels, who knows what will happen! Why did we bother risking our lives back in Constantinople if you were going to just give up like this?" Mus'ab spoke with assertiveness.

Jaffar kept his head lowered. "What do we do then, Mus'ab? She could have tossed that artifact anywhere. How can we possibly find it without any clues?"

"Okay, I don't think she would have tossed an ancient artifact away just like that. It's just too valuable, and she knows that. What did she say? Did she tell you anything?"

Jaffar shook his head. "Nothing."

Just then, Uncle Idrees walked up to the boys hurriedly. He adjusted the small rimless cap on top of his bald head breathing frantically.

"Jaffar! Mus'ab! You must go now and get the seventh artifact to the Jannah Jewels."

"But, Uncle. We don't have it!" Jaffar told him.

"Jasmin didn't tell you where it is?"

"No," replied Jaffar quietly.

"Do you at least know what it is?" asked his uncle.

"Yes, it's a *tasbih* that belonged to Sultan Muhammad II's father, which he gifted to us."

"A *tasbih*?" Uncle Idrees sounded alarmed. "Is it simple-looking with clear crystal beads?"

"Yes!" both Jaffar and Mus'ab hissed simultaneously.

"I was wondering where he got that from! Follow

me!"

The boys looked at each other in a puzzled manner. Then they quickly ran after Uncle Idrees who slammed open a staircase door and raced down two flights. The boys tried hard to keep his trail.

"Man, he's fast!" noted Mus'ab.

They arrived completely winded to the neurological intensive care unit. Uncle Idrees walked them to another patient's room. He knocked and entered the room quietly. Jaffar stayed close behind him, while Mus'ab waited outside again.

It was a small bare-walled room that smelled stuffy and hot, lit dimly by a florescent tube light above the patient's bed. There was no sunlight coming into the room as the windows were blocked by thick curtains. It was hard for Jaffar to see who was the thin, tall man lying asleep on the bed—his feet hanging over its edge.

Uncle Idrees grabbed hold of Jaffar's hand and led him closer to the bed. That is when Jaffar recognized the man's long boney face: it was Khan, his father. He was sleeping peacefully with his hands resting on his chest, and there, intertwined between his dry, frail fingers was the seventh artifact.

6

Royalty

"What if the eighth artifact is a giant marshmallow?" Jaide licked her lips as she sat under the tall oak tree sketching in her new sketchpad. "Or better yet...how about a bowl of fresh whipped cream?"

Iman cleared her throat. "Can we please focus here? I know you left Vancouver in the middle of your meal, but seriously? Whipped cream? You really think the ancient eighth artifact is going to be a dessert topping? And how is food an 'Opening'?" her tone was annoyed.

"Hey, you never know! Sensei said it was soft, white and fragile, which both a marshmallow and whipped cream fall under. Plus my stomach is always 'open' to food. Let's not rule out all our options here," Jaide protested. She looked over at Sara in hopes of some form of agreement from her, but Sara was too busy petting Shams in her lap.

"I feel so bad for Shams," said Sara, not realizing she changed the subject. "We were too busy training for the Turkey mission and weren't able to give her enough time and attention. Look at her." She lifted the weak goat's head and kissed it. "You poor baby," Sara said as she nuzzled up to her.

Hidayah listened quietly to the other Jewels. She was the only one standing out of the four to figure out where they had arrived and which direction they should head towards now. Her hand covered her eyes like a visor from the bright morning sun. All she could see for miles was open grassy fields.

"I don't see anyone around," she told her friends. "I have no idea where we are." She finally sat down next to the group and took out the ancient map from its bamboo case. She spread it open in the center of their circle. Laid out in front of them were images of 12 artifacts marked over various cities across the seven continents. Hidayah stared at the eighth image hovering over the southern central part of America, which looked to her like a white rectangular cloud.

"I highly doubt this is a marshmallow," Hidayah teased as she pointed it out on the map.

The girls all giggled except for Jaide.

"Fine. Whatever. We better find some food quick, because I'm starving," Jaide moaned putting her sketchpad away.

Shams let out a soft cry. She squeezed her eyes tightly a few times.

"So is she," Iman noted. "We need to find this 'Prince' and get his help right away. Shams looks like she might be in pain." She took the goat gently from Sara and wrapped her arms around her.

"What do you think the Prince looks like?" Sara asked with excitement as she stood up and dusted loose, dry grass off her clothes. "Do you think he lives in a palace? Maybe we will even get to meet a real live Princess!"

"Okay, that sounds even more ridiculous than

the ancient artifact being a marshmallow!" Jaide objected as she rolled her eyes. "We're in the middle of nowhere. I doubt we will find a giant palace here!"

Sara shrugged her shoulders. "You never know, okay?" She took a look around her surroundings. "It's so interesting to be in America. Were Muslims even part of American history?"

"Yeah, I was wondering the same thing. Let me check if I can find any info in the *Book of Knowledge*," suggested Iman as she struggled to pull the book out of her satchel one-handed.

Jaide quickly glanced at her wrist. "Hold that thought, Iman. I think we need to get moving. We've been here for over fifteen minutes already. Which way should we go?" she said.

Hidayah scanned their vicinity not knowing which way to head. *Ya Hadi, Our Lord, please guide us in the right direction.* She made a quiet prayer in her heart at that moment as she rolled up the map back into its case.

"Hey! Why don't we climb up this tree to get a better view of where we are?" said Sara. The girls had trained rigorously with Sara's mom, Mrs. Bellamy, before their Turkey mission. As Master Runner, she had taught them the art of parkour. "Jaide, come up with me," she ordered as she raced towards the oak tree and leaped up to climb it. Jaide followed right behind.

"See anything?" asked Hidayah from below.

Jaide and Sara searched the open fields from opposite sides of the tree.

"Look! There are some kids playing over there!" Jaide said as she pointed to some children in the far distance.

"Let's go!" Not wasting another minute, Hidayah jumped up and grabbed Iman's hand. They started running towards the direction Jaide had pointed. Sara and Jaide quickly climbed down and followed the other Jewels.

Soon they saw some children playing tag who suddenly froze as they caught sight of the four random girls coming towards them. "Run!" an older boy from the group shouted. They quickly turned and started to run away from the Jannah Jewels.

"Wait!" Hidayah screamed at the kids, but they picked up speed and kept running. Hidayah turned back and motioned to her friends. "Come on! Hurry!"

Warm air filled the girls' lungs as they charged after the other kids. Dry grass crunched under their feet. Iman held on tight to Shams as the goat bounced up and down in her arms.

The little children continued running until they reached an area full of tall oak trees. Shaded behind them was a small wooden cabin crowded with a slew of people busy in different affairs. An old lady sat on a tree stump separating vegetables into different containers.

Hidayah could see the kids run up to her and point in the Jewels' direction. The lady stood up and stretched her neck to look out to where the girls were. She wore a long dusty blue dress with a high ruffled collar that buttoned from the neck all the way down to the floor and a cream-colored apron tied around her waist. Her tethered dress grazed the unpaved ground as she walked gracefully towards the girls. The Jannah Jewels slowed their pace nearing her.

"May I help you?" the lady questioned. She was dark-skinned, with black and gray curly hair tied loosely under a white bonnet. She carried a pleasant disposition and greeted them with a subtle smile.

The Jannah Jewels were all out of breath and without words. Hidayah finally spoke up.

"Good morning, kind madam. We did not mean to startle the kids. We are here in search of a Prince in your area. Could you tell us where we can find him?"

The woman's face, which was sun-dried and full of wrinkles, became serious all of a sudden. "What matter do you have with him?"

Iman stepped forward with Shams. "We were told that he can help bring our goat back to health," she spoke with urgency.

The lady took a closer look at Shams. She petted her head gently. "She does not look well at all. Come with me."

As the Jannah Jewels followed her, the other working adults looked up and stared at them curiously. They were all dark-skinned like the old woman. She led them to the back of the cabin where there were some other small animals like chickens, ducks, and a few goats grazing inside a torn-metal fenced area. Some of the little children had come along with them and began to chase after loose chickens, then placed them back inside their coop.

"May I see her?" the lady asked reaching out her arms to Iman, who handed Shams to her. She carefully took the goat and lowered her into the fenced space. "Sameen! Susy! Fetch me a bowl of water! Quickly!" she ordered two kids that were nearest to her. Then she clucked her tongue calling the other goats. Two of her goats trotted towards her and pushed their noses against Shams side.

MAA! MAA!

"Aww. They are welcoming Shams," said Iman smiling.

The little boy named Sameen rushed over spilling some water as it splashed side-to-side in its bowl. Susy followed right behind him. "Here, *Jiddah*, my grandma," he said as he handed her the water. Shams quickly began to drink as the woman gave her the water.

Iman turned and looked down at Sameen. She crouched herself to be at his eye level. "You speak Arabic?" she questioned him with surprise.

"My grandfather has taught us a few words. His Arabic is *really* good!" the boy replied proudly.

Iman stood back up and turned to look at the other Jewels in a puzzled manner. "Arabic in America?" she whispered. The girls shrugged their shoulders as they were just as confused as her.

"What are your names?" the woman asked the Jewels.

"My name is Hidayah, and these are my friends Iman, Jaide, and Sara," she answered pointing to each.

The woman stared at Iman pensively. "And where are you from?"

"I'm from Canada, but my parents are from Guinea in West Africa."

"West Africa?" her old eyes suddenly lit up. "Is that near Futa Jallon?"

"That's what it was called in the paa-sst..." Iman immediately caught her words. "Yes, very close," she quickly corrected herself and smiled. "Are you from there too?"

The crow's feet at the corners of the old woman's eyes bunched together as she began to tear up. "No," she answered softly. "But the Prince is. He will be so pleased to meet you. It's been so long."

The Jannah Jewels all exchanged confused glances with each other.

"Can you take us to him please?" Hidayah politely asked.

"He is preparing to oversee the morning harvest," she said as she wiped her eyes with her apron. "The new crops of the season are ready, but they are very hard to pick. He will return shortly to gather his children to help him. Those were the folks you saw up front preparing to head out with him," she informed the Jewels.

"And how do you know the Prince?" asked Sara.

The elderly woman smiled with content. "I am blessed to be his wife, Izzah."

The Jewels stared at her in disbelief. Izzah looked nothing like a real-life Princess.

7

Prince or Slave?

"Izzah! Izzah! Where are you?" a man's deep, course voice called out from afar.

"Back here, Prince! In the barn area!" she shouted back.

A tall elderly man with copper-colored skin walked out from around the corner of the log house towards Izzah and the Jannah Jewels. A trail of little kids followed after him. Despite his old age, he was an impressive-looking man with a long, thin face, a broad nose, a wide forehead and thick lips. He was of a powerful frame and well-proportioned. Dressed simply in a white cotton shirt, he wore patched-up khaki trousers with rugged, worn-out boots underneath. His frizzy white hair had hints of black in it and stood up all over his head. His dark eyes fell upon the Jewels as he took long upright strides over to them. There was a look of wonder in his gaze.

Hidayah could not help but think how opposite of royalty he looked compared to Sultan Muhammad II, who they had just met back in Turkey, or King Mansa Musa back in Mali. Yet, he still carried himself in such a dignified manner and had an illuminating presence to him.

As the Prince drew near, he then gave the Jannah Jewels a welcoming smile. He placed his right hand on his heart and greeted the girls with *salaam*, peace. "My name is Ibrahima Abdur Rahman. To what do I owe this great honor?"

The girls all blushed shyly. "Peace be upon you too," they each replied, introducing themselves individually.

"Prince, these young ladies have come in hopes of bringing their sick goat back to health with your help," Izzah told him.

He turned and looked at where Shams was

grazing. "Is that her?" he asked.

"Yes," replied Iman.

Prince walked over to Shams and picked her up examining her carefully. "You are beautiful," he told her as he stroked her coat softly. "Where is she from?" he questioned.

"Morocco," Iman told him.

"Africa," he whispered as if talking to himself. "I am from Africa too," he then told the Jewels. He squeezed the goat against his chest as if to hug her. "It feels like you all have brought a piece of home for me," he said with satisfaction.

Hidayah's heart sank for a moment. *Is Shams the gift we must give to this Prince?* she worried, since the goat never really was the Jewels' to begin with as she belonged to Mus'ab.

"When did you come to America?" Sara questioned the Prince interrupting Hidayah's thought.

The Prince took a deep breath. "Almost 40 years ago," he answered with heaviness. His eyes carried a distant look in them. "I was a Prince and a colonel

back in my homeland of Futa Jallon before I was captured and forced to cross the Atlantic. I was then brought to Natchez, Mississippi and sold here as a slave."

A look of realization came over each of the Jannah Jewels' faces. This noble Prince had lived the majority of his life as a slave.

"I would never have imagined my life to have become what it did. These last four decades have been very difficult. I was taken from my family, tortured and abused, and used to do such hard labor—all against my will," the Prince told the Jewels, who stared at him solemnly. He then noticed their sad disposition. "However, God places you where He sees best. I met Izzah here, and we have been blessed with nine wonderful children. As a slave family, we have worked very hard to cultivate this land. Despite all our hardship, I have held on tight to my faith, which has gotten me through it all. Perhaps God wanted Islam to reach this New World."

"Prince, Iman's family comes from Futa Jallon too," his wife told him in a comforting manner.

Prince Ibrahima's dark eyes shined bright with joy. "Is this true?!" he asked with excitement.

Iman nodded with a smile.

"Glory be to God!" he exclaimed. "My old eyes have tired waiting to see someone from my homeland. Is your family safe and free?" he asked Iman.

"Yes, there is no slavery where we live," she reassured him.

"You must be from the north colony then," the Prince assumed.

MAA!

Before Iman could respond, Shams squirmed within Prince Ibrahima's arms. He then carefully placed her back down to graze again.

"She sure is hungry!" he laughed.

All the Jewels giggled and were pleased to see Shams starting to act like herself again.

"Wow, I'm surprised she's eating again," Iman noted. "Shams has been resisting food and drink for some time with us."

"*Shams*...which means 'sun' in Arabic. What a suiting name for her: orange like the sun," the Prince translated.

"You are fluent in Arabic?" asked Jaide.

"Yes, and I know five other languages as well," he told them proudly. "I began my studies at age 7 and mastered *Qur'anic* Arabic by age 12. My father, the king, then sent me to the magnificent city of Timbuktu from our town of Timbo until I was the age of 17. It was much more sophisticated and advanced than what I have seen here."

At the mention of Timbuktu, each of the Jewels recalled their very first mission there saving the ancient manuscripts. It was indeed a spectacular city where they met the great King Mansa Musa.

"It was two months travel by land," Prince Ibrahima continued. "We had over two hundred students in our school where we learned subjects like geography, astronomy, calculations, the Islamic sciences such as sayings of Prophet Muhammad, peace and blessings be upon him, jurisprudence, languages of the countries with which we traded, and the laws of our land. I miss my days in Africa, my people, and my mosque set amongst the orange trees so much," he said with grief in his voice, his eyes looking misty.

Even with the hustle and bustle around them, the air grew silent. The Jewels all listened to Prince Ibrahima wholeheartedly but were at a loss of words. They realized that in front of them stood a Muslim Prince in America, yet wrongfully enslaved.

Suddenly, Shams let out another cry.

MAA!

"I think I know what is wrong with Shams," Prince said.

"What?!" Iman asked with anticipation.

"She is homesick," he answered. "Just like me."

8

The Eighth Artifact

And just like that, the Jannah Jewels became overwhelmed with guilt.

"We shouldn't have kept her," Iman realized sadly.

"Goats are very social creatures," informed the Prince. "Look at how she is interacting with our goats here. She must have been missing her owner and the rest of her herd," he speculated. "Has she had company around her?"

"Not as of late," Hidayah replied with a heavy heart.

"And you say she was not eating much...what did she used to eat in Morocco?" Prince Ibrahima asked.

They all thought hard for a moment. Jaide's stomach grumbled. She then remembered how hungry she was just like when they first arrived back in Morocco under the argan tree that was full of grazing goats.

"Oh! Argan fruit!" she suddenly recalled.

"She hasn't had that since she came back with us," noted Sara.

"Do you have that fruit up north?" Prince asked them.

"No," said Hidayah.

"You must take her back then at once," he spoke with urgency.

The girls all glanced at each other with looks of concern.

How will we ever be able to do that? Hidayah wondered.

A man came running up to the Prince right then.

"Father! We are ready when you are."

"I'll be right there," he told him.

"Picking the harvest is very difficult," Prince informed the Jewels.

"May we come help?" asked Iman. The other Jewels nodded in agreement.

Prince Ibrahima shook his head. "No, I would never wish the work of a slave upon anyone," he objected. "You may come see the new harvest, though, if you like. It's definitely a sight to see," he invited them with a small smile.

"Let them eat something first," Izzah insisted. "You all get going. I'll bring these girls to the plantation after they have a bite to eat," she told him.

As Prince left with his family, the Jewels noticed how his daughters and many of his grandchildren went with him to pick the harvest. Hidayah, Iman, Jaide and Sara exchanged gloomy looks with each other.

"You all look like you could really use some nourishment," Izzah noted. "Follow me."

Izzah led the girls into her log house through a

hinged door. The cozy house smelled of fresh timber and was made of wood, stone and mud. There were holes in the roof, windows made of greased paper and a dirt floor. A blackened fireplace covered in old soot was in the center of a long wall, and a small cast-iron stove sat humbly in one corner with a pot cooking over its grate. It was hotter inside the house from the heat of the stove. Besides a few furnishings like some wooden shelves, trunks and a short table with four chairs, the space was rather empty. Hidayah noticed something that looked like a sheep-skin mat spread in one corner. She wondered if it was a prayer rug or a sleeping mat.

"Please have a seat," Izzah politely said pointing to the table.

As the girls sat down, their chairs creaked underneath them. They looked around the small home and marveled at how neatly it was kept.

"Do you *all* live in here?" Jaide asked puzzled. Sara quickly kicked her in the leg from below the table popping her eyes out at Jaide. She quietly mouthed her to shush. "I mean—this is really nice!"

Jaide corrected herself, her cheeks flushing with redness.

Izzah let out a subtle laugh. "Why thank you! And no, my dear, don't be silly. We all don't live in here, only Prince and I. Most of the kids are married and have their own log homes with their families around here. Prince and his sons worked hard to build 'em all." She wiped the table with a wet cloth then grabbed some clay round bowls from the shelves and walked over to the stove. She poured hot, chunky liquid into each of the four bowls and brought them over to the Jewels.

"Drink up now. You need all the energy you can get."

Each of the girls' mouths watered at the sight of the steaming stew: its warm aroma of hearty, cooked vegetables seeped up into their happy noses. They quietly recited the eating supplication and began taking small sips at a time.

"Mmm, Ms. Izzah, this is absolutely delicious," said Jaide, who was now chugging down the hot stew.

"All Praise be to God," she thanked. "Once you ladies are done, feel free to wash up out back. You'll see the well out there," she pointed to a small door that was ajar behind her. "I'm going to pack some snacks to take to the family."

Hidayah, Iman, Jaide and Sara drank to their fullest. They picked up their bowls and walked out back quietly together.

"It's so beautiful out here," said Sara, who loved being outdoors and in nature. "The air feels so clean and light." She closed her eyes and took a deep breath in through her nose.

As they reached the well, Hidayah pulled up a bucket of fresh water with the pulley. There was a clay cup inside, which they used to pour water to rinse their bowls. Then they sat and drank some water together.

"Iman, can you look in your *Book of Knowledge* now and find some information about Prince Ibrahima and where we are?" Hidayah asked. As Iman grabbed the book from her satchel, Hidayah then turned and looked at Jaide. "And how are we

77

doing on time?"

Jaide glanced at her watch. "We have less than four hours."

"How should we go about this, girls?" Hidayah asked the Jewels. "We need to get Shams back to Mus'ab somehow, but he and Jaffar haven't shown up here yet. Plus we don't know if they found the seventh artifact or not. Aside from that, we still need to find the eighth artifact, plus give the Prince a gift—which we don't have either." The other Jewels could sense some worry in Hidayah's voice.

"Iman? Did you find anything?" Sara asked hoping for some direction.

Iman was scanning through the pages very quickly. Her eyes lit up wide behind her glasses as she silently read more and more, her smile growing bigger and bigger. "Oh mi gosh!" She placed the book onto the grass and quickly jumped up, lifting her skirt and running rapidly back to the log house.

"Where are you going?!" Hidayah called after her, but Iman kept running.

She popped her head into the log house for a

minute and then ran right back. Hidayah, Jaide and Sara looked up at her with their eyes squinted as the sun shined brightly above them.

Iman took a moment to catch her breath before she spoke. "I just asked Ms. Izzah what year it is," panted Iman.

"Didn't she think that was a weird question?!" Jaide asked with curiosity.

"No. Not really. Anyway, the good news is that it's 1826!" The girls all stared at Iman in silence.

"And?!" questioned Jaide.

"And!—that's only three years before Prince is freed and returns to Africa!" Iman clapped her hands together and hopped up and down with excitement.

Hidayah, Jaide and Sara all sprouted up and started screaming with delight. The Jewels then huddled up for a group hug jumping ecstatically. A bunch of Prince's little grandchildren had now crowded around them completely baffled. The girls all laughed together when they saw the kids staring at them.

"Sorry. Didn't mean to startle you all," Iman said kindly. "You all run along now," and the kids went back to playing.

"This is amazing! We have to tell him!" suggested Sara.

"Read us what it says, Iman," said Hidayah.

They all sat back down in a circle. Iman put the book back in her lap on top of her skirt that stretched over her knees as she read aloud, *"After 40 years of enslavement, Prince Ibrahima Abdur Rahman crossed the Atlantic Ocean once again, but this time as a freed man on a passenger ship named the* Harriet. *On March 18, 1829, he finally returned to Africa with his wife."*

"Oh mi gosh! I think I'm going to cry!" Sara waved her hands in front of her eyes. "This is absolutely amazing. Let's go tell him right now!"

The Jewels happily gathered their things and hurried back to the log house. Izzah was stuffing a basket with bread, vegetables, and fruit.

"Ms. Izzah! Ms. Izzah! Can you take us to the plantation now?" Hidayah asked hastily.

"Yes, let's head over," she replied.

Hidayah's eyes then fell upon a pile of paper scraps on the shelf behind Izzah. She walked up to the shelf to take a closer look. "May I see these?" she kindly asked Izzah.

"Yes, but be very careful. They are a prized position of the Prince's."

Hidayah reached up and gently pulled the small torn papers down from the shelf. Her eyes spread open wide and her mouth stretched into an astonished smile as she flipped through the papers.

"Girls. I found...the Opening!" Hidayah lifted a tiny piece of paper with Arabic writing on it and showed it to the other Jewels. The cabin grew quiet.

Iman, Jaide, and Sara slowly headed over to where Hidayah stood.

"It's the 'Opening' to the *Qur'an!*" Iman realized. The girls were amazed to see the first chapter of the *Holy Book* beautifully written out by hand on the small sheet.

"Yes, Prince likes to write down verses of the

Qur'an," explained Izzah. "He wants to make sure he always remembers God's words."

"Glory be to God," spoke Sara. "The *Qur'an* has been in America for such a long time."

Izzah questioningly stared at Sara.

"What she means is that since Prince Ibrahima has been here for forty years, then he has kept the *Qur'an* with him for such a long time," Hidayah quickly corrected. "Do you think he would let us take this?" she asked Izzah diverting her attention.

"That is up to him," she stated. "We can ask him. Come along now," she said in an easy-going manner as they all headed out of the log house. They walked through large fields for quite some time taking in the beautiful open sky.

Izzah looked over at Hidayah. "You use that for hunting?" she gestured with her eyes towards the large red bow on Hidayah's back.

"Oh, this? It's more for protection, I guess," replied Hidayah.

"Prince taught me how to use one too," Izzah told

her proudly. "He is amazing with a bow and arrow."

"Really?" Hidayah said. "I would love to learn some pointers from each of you."

"We'd be honored. After the plantation, let's go catch some fresh catfish in the Mississippi River for lunch."

Jaide's ears stood up at the word 'lunch.' She walked up closer to Izzah and Hidayah. "Did someone say 'lunch'?" the food-lover asked as she licked her lips.

Hidayah turned back to smile at Jaide. "That sounds great, Ms. Izzah," she then thanked.

As they approached the plantation shortly thereafter, the Jannah Jewels eyes lit up in amazement. They arrived at acres and acres of white, fluffy fibers covering the plants. The land glistened in the sunlight. It looked as if the clouds had descended and spread themselves like soft balls all over the vast fields.

"Whoaaaa!" said Jaide. "We found the marshmallows," she whispered with delight.

Izzah laughed. "These are not marshmallow plants. They are cotton plants, my dear."

The Jewels paused their steps and stared out into the field. *Could this be the eighth artifact instead?* each of them wondered.

9

Freedom

"Wait. Is this the eighth artifact?" Sara questioned the others.

"I don't know, but I want to touch it," stated Jaide. "It looks so beautiful!"

"Go right ahead," Izzah answered.

Jaide ran up to a plant and felt the fiber between her fingers. It was extremely soft and cushion-like. "It may not be marshmallows," noted Jaide, "but now I have a craving for cotton candy," she said with a smile.

"Okay, I'll admit—all your food talk is making me hungry too. Cut it out," Iman said laughingly. She then looked up and saw how hard the Prince's family was working in the fields. Each member, young and old, was meticulously hand-picking the cotton, some carrying heavy loads on their backs. The sun seemed lower on their sweaty heads and fatigue was very visible on their faces. Iman's smile quickly faded at the sight of the working slave family.

Just then, Prince Ibrahima walked up wearing a sunhat on his head. "Welcome," he greeted.

"This is absolutely incredible, Sir," Hidayah praised. "You and your family have really worked hard to grow all this cotton."

"Yes. Yes, we have. The plantation's owner, Mr. Foster, put me in charge of the fields decades ago. At first, I refused. I even ran away in search of my freedom again. After weeks of being stranded in the wilderness all alone and nowhere else to go, I had no choice but to come back and succumb to my life as a slave." The Jewels listened attentively to the Prince's story.

Prince Ibrahima took a deep sigh. "Lucky for Mr. Foster, I happened to be very familiar with the cotton seed and its plant back in Futa Jallon," he then told them. "You need lots of sunshine, water, and fertile soil to make the plant grow. However, there is also something special I used for these fields of white gold," the Prince added.

"What's that?" Iman asked.

"God's name and *du'a*," he said with a grin.

The Jannah Jewels all smiled at his words. The blessings were apparent in the cotton plant's abundance.

Sara leaned into Hidayah's ear. "Let's just go home now," she whispered.

Hidayah shook her head. "Not yet," she whispered back. "We haven't given him a gift yet nor received the seventh artifact from Jaffar and Mus'ab."

Sara then carried an expression of realization.

"Prince, Hidayah was wondering if you could help her improve her archery skills," spoke Izzah. "I thought we could take them to the river to catch some fish."

"Why, yes, of course," Prince Ibrahima replied.

"Let me hand over these snacks to the family first," he said as he took the basket from Izzah.

The girls watched as the Abdur Rahman family quickly ate and then went back to picking the cotton. They each carefully pulled the cotton lock off its burr which was attached to a tall brown stalk. Prince then walked back with the emptied basket.

"Shall we?" he asked gesturing the group to follow his lead.

"Wait. Before we go, we wanted to ask you something, Sir." Hidayah told him. She was not sure what the eighth artifact was now: the hand-written first chapter of the *Qur'an* called *Surah Al-Fatiha* or the cotton plant.

"If you don't mind, can we keep this?" Hidayah asked as she pulled out the fragile little paper from her pocket. "It would mean so much to us."

The Prince smiled. "I pray the power of these verses brings many openings into each of your lives. Of course you may keep it."

Hidayah then realized that *Surah Al-Fatiha* must be the true eighth artifact.

The other Jannah Jewels' eyes shined bright, but Hidayah hesitated a bit.

"I'm sorry, but we have nothing to offer you in place of it," she told him.

"Oh, but we do!" Iman quickly chimed in. "We come with glad tidings, Prince Ibrahima, that one day in the near future you will be freed, God-willing!" she said as she beamed a huge smile at him.

Prince Ibrahima and Izzah stood stunned, their expressions frozen. This was not at all how the Jewels expected them to react.

"And who will free me?" the Prince asked with seriousness. "Mr. Foster will never agree. My old friend from Africa, Dr. Cox, who I coincidently reunited with here in Natchez, was not able to buy my freedom despite his and his family's relentless efforts."

The girls remained quiet. Iman thought hard for a minute. "He will agree if the American government tells him to free you."

The Prince dropped his jaw. He looked at Izzah in shock and then back at Iman. Izzah stayed solemn and motionless.

"The American government? How can that be? My hairs have turned white like the cotton I've sowed over these last few decades. No one from the government is coming to free me," his tone was very matter-of-fact.

No one knew what to say. The air grew thick with silence.

"Could you maybe write a letter in Arabic?" Izzah suddenly spoke up.

"In Arabic?" Prince contemplated the idea. "You think that might work?" his voice carried a sense of optimism.

"You write so well," Hidayah answered. She then pulled out the tiny paper from her pocket with the *Qur'anic* verses written on it. "This is proof," she showed him.

Izzah grabbed the Prince's hand with both of hers. Her eyes were full of hope as she smiled faintly. "I believe them, Prince. You deserve to be free. It's definitely worth trying. Maybe Mr. Marschalk from the local newspaper can help you somehow. He seems to have a real liking for you and knows you can read and write in Arabic."

Prince Ibrahima began to nod slowly. "You are right, Izzah. It is worth a try. By Allah's will, I shall do it then." He then turned and smiled at the Jewels. "All praise be to God! You four have brought such light with you by giving me this renewed gift of hope. May He shower you with His Goodness."

"*Ameen*," the girls hummed together with joy.

10

Go Fish

The Jannah Jewels enjoyed the rest of the morning with Prince and Izzah and some of their grandchildren. The air was much cooler by the river. Iman, Jaide and Sara sat with the kids and watched as Prince Ibrahima helped Hidayah sharpen her archery skills. He even showed her how to catch some catfish.

"They move fast, so you must be quick without much movement. Otherwise you will startle the fish," he told her. "Be still, focus, and then aim at the spot where you think the fish will swim towards. Beat the fish at its own game," he instructed.

A moving fish seemed like a very difficult target to Hidayah. She had never tried catching one with her arrow before.

Izzah placed her hand on Hidayah's shoulder. "Don't aim with your eyes. Aim with your heart," she told her.

Izzah's words reminded Hidayah of Sensei Elle. She had told Hidayah that a good archer can shoot even with her eyes closed.

With both of their words in mind, Hidayah closed her eyes and listened. The sound of the water flowing over the rocks in the river calmed her. A small current kept the water moving freely. She listened carefully for any change in the splashing of the liquid. From her right ear, she sensed a sudden change in motion. The water was carrying a weight with it. She turned her body slowly towards its direction and lowered her bow and arrow. She could hear the movement in the water coming closer to her. She pulled her right hand back as she stretched the bow and aimed her arrow downwards.

Wait for it. Wait for it. It's coming. It's coming... *Bismillah!* Hidayah released the arrow and heard it pierce through the air. She opened her eyes and saw a blue catfish planted against a rock, its fin still fluttering.

The Jannah Jewels and all the little children cheered.

"Glory be to God!" shouted Prince Ibrahima. "That was amazing!"

Izzah yanked out the arrow and quickly placed the fish in her basket. "I knew you could do it!" she told Hidayah.

"Thank you," Hidayah said humbly.

"Now who wants lunch?" Izzah grinned.

Jaide shot her arm in the air.

"Great. Come help me quickly gather some firewood then."

"Sure!" Jaide responded enthusiastically. She rose and walked around the grassy shore with Izzah.

"If you search the ground below the trees, you'll find tons of loose sticks and branches," Izzah advised, but Jaide did not seem to find any that way.

She glanced at her time-traveling watch. They only had 90 minutes left. "Can I just climb up this tree and pull off some branches instead?" Jaide asked to hurry things along. Plus, she was really hungry.

"Oh, these old legs of mine aren't made for climbing anymore. You go right ahead, honey. Just be careful," said Izzah.

Jaide carefully climbed up the thick trunk and sat onto a wide, sturdy branch. The view from atop was serene. Jaide could see for miles down the empty shore lined with beautiful shades of green.

She yanked small twigs and thin branches off and tossed them gently down. As she took in the scenery, she suddenly noticed a young boy in the distance bobbing in and out of the water. He was gasping for air waving his arms frantically. Another boy was lying on his stomach on the shore reaching out to help him but was too far. Jaide recognized the curly-haired boy on the shore: it was Mus'ab.

"Somebody help us!!!" she barely heard Mus'ab scream the words from afar.

Jaide hopped off the tree branch tumbling into a ball as she hit the grass. She stood up frantically.

"Mus'ab needs our help! Jaffar's drowning!" her

words trailed off as she raced down the shore. Even without her skateboard, she could pick up great speed on her feet.

The Jewels quickly sprouted up and chased after her. The boys were across the opposite side of the river. The girls had no way to get to them by land. As they reached closer, Hidayah saw Jaffar panting for air. She remembered how she rescued him out of the ocean back in China, but she could not figure out how to help him now.

"Help!" the words bubbled out of Jaffar's mouth. He was fighting for his life.

"Quick! What do we do?" Iman asked in a panic.

Sara did not waste another minute. She knew what she had to do. She threw off her slippers and dived into the cold river.

"Sara! No!" Hidayah yelled after her, but Sara was already side-breathing and cutting through the slow-moving current. She was the best swimmer out of the four.

She reached Jaffar in no time and grabbed hold of the back of his robe. She yanked him behind her

as she swam over to the shore. Mus'ab helped pull Jaffar ashore as Sara dragged herself out of the water.

She was completely soaked and out of breath. Sara lay on her back trying to suck in pockets of clean air. She then turned and looked at Jaffar. He was not moving.

"Jaffar! Jaffar! Wake up!" she shouted, but he remained still. "No, please, Allah, please!" She quickly stood up, water dripping from every inch of her clothes and her *hijab* plastered to her head. "Mus'ab, do something!"

Mus'ab shook Jaffar profusely. "Dude! Wake up!" He slapped Jaffar's face, but it was no use. Jaffar lay still. "I don't know what to do!" Mus'ab was frantic with fear for his best friend's life.

Sara then saw the Prince standing on a wooden raft paddling his way down the river towards them. "Prince Ibrahima! Over here!" Sara waved her arms to and fro. "Hurry! He's not moving!" she screamed.

Prince paddled faster and his raft met the shore in no time. He jumped off and ran up to Jaffar immediately flipping him over onto his stomach. He repeatedly pushed down on Jaffar's back and slapped it hard. "Breathe, boy, breathe! O Allah, help us!" he prayed.

Jaffar suddenly began coughing out water. Prince Ibrahima, Sara and Mus'ab sighed with relief and thankfulness.

"*Alhamdullilah!*" cheered the Prince. He turned back towards the others standing on the opposite shore and gave them an 'okay' sign. He then helped Jaffar sit up slowly.

"What were you doing in that cold river?" asked Prince.

"Sir, we were lost and had been running up and down this shore trying to find a way around the river for hours. Then Jaffar just bent down to grab a drink of some fresh water and next thing we knew, he was in the river," Mus'ab answered.

"Your name is Jaffar?"

Jaffar nodded, still slightly dazed.

"Jaffar." The Prince said the name with

satisfaction and looked at him with content. "Do you know who you are named after?"

"Yes," Jaffar nodded as he shivered. "My mother named me after the cousin and close companion of Prophet Muhammad, peace and blessings be upon him."

"Yes, his name was Jaffar ibn Abi Talib, and he was amongst those who migrated to Abyssinia from Makkah and helped bring Islam to Africa, may Allah be pleased with him," shared Prince Ibrahima. "You never know where God will place you. Where ever it may be, know you must continue God's work and exemplify the character of His beloved Prophet, peace and blessings be upon him," he advised Jaffar, Mus'ab and Sara.

Jaffar's teeth clattered. "Yes, Sir."

"Jaffar, this is Prince Ibrahima Abdur Rahman of Futa Jallon, West Africa," Sara introduced. "And Prince Ibrahima, this is Jaffar and Mus'ab of Morocco, North Africa."

The Prince gave both the boys a warm, pleasing smile. "Welcome." He then carefully helped Jaffar to his feet. "Come. We must get you some dry clothes," he insisted. He signaled Izzah and the other Jewels on the opposite shore to head back too.

The walk back to the log house was far away. As they walked together, the Prince kept his arm around Jaffar to keep him warm. Sara kept her arms crossed as best as she could to warm herself. The heat from the zenith sun was definitely helping dry her off. She lagged slightly behind the boys.

Mus'ab was fascinated with the Prince's story and asked him questions one after another. Jaffar turned back to see how far Sara was. He let the Prince and Mus'ab match paces as he waited for Sara to catch up.

"You okay?" he asked as she neared.

She nodded with her gaze down. It was still hard for Sara to face Jaffar.

"I can't thank you enough for saving me back there. You didn't have to do that," he sincerely spoke.

Sara remained quiet for a minute. She then knew this might be her only chance to finally face her guilt.

"I did have to," she responded.

He glanced at her in a puzzled manner.

"It's the least I can do after what I did to your father," the words were hard for her to release.

"Oh," he suddenly realized what she meant.

"Please forgive me, Jaffar. It was the only thing I could do at the time to save us. Your father really scared us back in Fes," Sara tried to justify her actions.

Jaffar's expression was neutral. He did not respond.

Sara then continued, "How is he now? Is he okay?"

"No," Jaffar paused and lowered his gaze. "My uncle visits him regularly and told me my father has lost his memory after the concussion. He wakes up frightened and confused, so the doctors keep him sedated. They don't know how long it will take for him to get better." He spoke with heaviness.

Sara's heart hurt. "I am so sorry to hear that. I will continue making *du'a* for him."

The rest of the way, they walked in silence. When they reached Prince's home, Izzah gave Jaffar and Sara some fresh clothes. Meanwhile, Hidayah, Iman and Jaide led Mus'ab to the small barn behind the log house.

"Mus'ab, close your eyes. We have a surprise for you," Jaide told him.

He gave her a suspicious look but then did as she asked. The Prince's grandson Sameen pulled him by the hand towards the fenced area of the loud blaring goats.

"Okay, now open!"

Mus'ab's eyes fell immediately upon Shams. "Is that my Shams?!" he asked stunned. He leaped over the metal fence and grabbed his beloved goat into his arms. "Oh, Shams, where have you been? We missed you so much! We've been going crazy looking for you!" He squeezed her tight and kissed her head.

"We are so sorry, Mus'ab," Iman apologized. "She somehow followed us back to Canada through your argan tree. We thought it was okay to keep her, but she has been quite homesick since she left you. Prince Ibrahima made us realize that. He says she needs to go home," she told him with a heavy heart.

"We all do," said Jaide looking at her watch. "It's almost time," she told the gang.

Hidayah quickly felt her jacket's pocket for the little piece of paper. It was still safe inside. She then remembered the seventh artifact.

"Mus'ab, were you and Jaffar able to find Jasmin and retrieve the stolen artifact?"

Musab's curly hair fell over his face as he looked down to the side of his robe. "Yes," he replied reaching into his pocket and pulling out the crystal *tasbih*.

The Jannah Jewels were all relieved to have it back. Hidayah carefully took it and placed it safely in her pocket along with the 'Opening.'

Such lightweight artifacts, yet so important, she thought to herself.

"Prince Ibrahima and Ms. Izzah, thank you for everything. May Allah free you both soon," Sara prayed.

"Be safe, my children," said Prince Ibrahima. "And may you all continue shining for others."

The girls hugged Izzah as she kissed each of their heads. "It's a shame we couldn't enjoy that big catfish together," she told them with disappointment.

"I'm sure your family will enjoy it more," said Jaide with a smile.

The Jewels then walked over to Mus'ab, who was holding Shams in his arms. They each petted her head, their hearts heavy and sad.

"We will miss you so much, Shamsu," Iman teared as she kissed the goat's head. "Go home and be happy," she told her with a reluctant smile.

MAA!

Hidayah then looked at Jaffar and Mus'ab. "You guys really risked your lives bringing back the seventh artifact. We couldn't have done it without you."

"Anything to help the Jannah Jewels save the world," Jaffar grinned.

"You know I'm always up for an adventure!" said Mus'ab with enthusiasm. "Hey, speaking of which, where's my skateboard by the way?"

Jaide cringed. "Yeah…umm…about that. I left it at home, because we were short on time. I promise I'll bring it next time, okay?"

Mus'ab squinted his eyes and bunched his lips. "I'm going to hold you to that," he then smiled.

"Until next time then," said Hidayah.

"God-willing," added Jaffar.

The six friends bid farewell and then went their separate ways.

"We have less than 10 minutes, girls," Jaide noted.

Hidayah quickly pulled out her ancient compass to help direct them back to the original oak tree where they had arrived. The Jewels ran swiftly through the open fields, the warm sun leading the way.

"Ready?" Hidayah asked standing next to the dark trunk of the oak tree, her voice was peaceful and satiated.

106

Iman, Jaide and Sara nodded smilingly. "Ready," they all responded.

The Jannah Jewels pushed the oak tree as hard as they could and down, down, down they went sliding through the tunnel.

When they reached the bottom, they locked hands and recited in unison, *"Bismillah hir Rahman nir Raheem!"*

11

Home

There was a great whirring sound. They opened their eyes to the warmth of their favorite misty maple tree. The air smelled sweet and welcoming. The lanterns were dimly lit and all was quiet.

The Jewels heard multiple footsteps coming towards them through one of the underground tunnels. One-by-one, the Four Masters entered lighting up the inside of the tree with their radiant smiles.

"Peace be upon each of you and welcome back," Sensei Elle greeted them.

"Peace be upon you too," the girls replied beaming with happiness.

They took turns hugging the Master Archer, Master Rider, Master Artist and Master Swimmer.

"It's so nice to see you all together," Hidayah told them.

"We have been praying for you four to return home safely," said Sensei Elle. "How was your mission?"

"Alhamdullilah, we were able to bring back both the seventh and eighth artifacts, Dear Masters," Hidayah told them gratefully.

"Come. Let's place them into the Golden Clock at once then," Sensei Elle instructed.

Hidayah pulled out the two artifacts and handed the tasbih to Iman. Together they walked over to the large Clock. Iman first laid the crystal-beaded tasbih gently inside the empty space at the hour of seven o'clock. Hidayah then placed the small paper of Qur'an at the hour of eight o'clock. The walls of the inside of the maple tree glowed from the bright light of the Golden Clock. The two artifacts were accepted and fit perfectly.

"Congratulations, Jannah Jewels. You did it

again," said Sensei Elle.

The girls all hugged and cheered with excitement.

"Each of you showed great strength and courage on these last two missions," the Master Swimmer spoke. "Sara, you showed beautiful courage when you saved Jaffar from drowning. You have worked hard to overcome your fear of dark waters. Well done."

"*Alhamdulillah* – thank you, Master Swimmer," said Sara, as a shy smile appeared on her face.

"Iman, you have been communicating with animals beautifully like Shuja'ah, the hawk, in Turkey and Shams, the goat, on this last mission. I know it must have been so hard for you to let her go, but it was the right thing to do," spoke Master Rider.

"Yes…it was, but thank you so much," Iman said softly.

"God sees your efforts and sacrifice. Here, take this and use it to help you understand the animal world of Allah even better," the Master Rider said as she handed Iman a nicely-wrapped gift.

"For me?" her expression brightened.

Master Rider smiled and nodded.

The other Jewels watched with anticipation as Iman quickly unwrapped her present. She gasped with delight as she held a new book in her hands.

"*The Great Book of How to Communicate with Animals*?! Oh mi gosh! I've been wanting to get my hands on this for-EVER! Thank you! Thank you! Thank you!" she hugged Master Rider tightly.

"May Allah accept all your hard work, Jewels." Sensei prayed. "You girls deserve a nice break. Now go rest," she told them.

Sensei Elle and the other Masters then said *salaam* and walked out through one of the underground tunnels.

"Okay, are you guys ready to hear my big plan?" Jaide asked as she and the Jewels headed home in the late afternoon.

"What?" Hidayah asked.

"Step one: eat food. Step two: take a warm bath. Step three: sleep!"

The girls all laughed hard.

"Sounds like the perfect plan!" said Sara.

Together, the Jannah Jewels then hurried down their street—happy to be home again.

Don't miss the next Jannah Jewels book!

Will the Jannah Jewels be able to find the ninth artifact? Will Jasmin recover and seek her revenge? Will Mus'ab and Jaffar be able to help the Jewels again? Will Khan ever be able to find Layla? Will the intruders strike again?

Find out in the next exciting adventure of the Jannah Jewels: "Surprise in Syria."

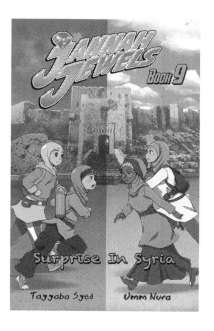

Find out more about the ninth book by visiting our website at **www.JannahJewels.com**

Glossary

Abyssinia: a country in Africa known as modern day Ethiopia

Alhamdullilah: Arabic for 'All praise is for God'

Allah: Arabic for 'God'

Ameen: same as 'Amen,' it is the Arabic word to close a supplication

Bismillah: Arabic for 'in the name of God'

Bismillah hir Rahman nir Raheem: Arabic for 'in the name of God, The Most Gracious, The Most Merciful'

Du'a: Arabic for 'supplication'

In sha Allah: Arabic for 'God-willing'

Jiddah: Arabic for 'grandmother'

Makkah: sacred city in Saudi Arabia where Islam began

Qur'an: sacred scripture of Islam

Salaam: a greeting in Arabic meaning 'peace'

Surah Al-Fatiha: The first chapter in the Holy Qur'an

which means 'The Opening.'

Tasbih: a string of beads tied together to help keep count of one's supplications

Ya Hadi: a name of God in Arabic meaning 'The Guide'

IMAN

SARA

To find out more about our other books,

go to:

www.JannahJewels.com